Keeping Cool

How you sweat, shiver, and keep warm

Steve Parker

FRANKLIN WATTS
New York • London • Toronto • Sydney

© 1992 Franklin Watts

Franklin Watts, Inc.
95 Madison Avenue
New York, NY 10016

Library of Congress Cataloging-in-Publication Data

Parker, Steve.
    Keeping cool / by Steve Parker.
        p.   cm. — (Body in Action)
    Includes bibliographical references and index.
    Summary: explains how the body reacts to changing conditions such
as temperature or humidity, how it adapts to its surroundings, and
how the skin protects the body from harmful sun rays.
    ISBN 0-531-14147-0
    1. Body temperature—Juvenile literature.   [1. Body temperature.]
I. Title.
QP82.2.T4P37   1992
612'.022—dc20   91-42675
                                                           CIP AC

Printed in Great Britain

Medical consultant: Dr. Puran Ganeri, MBBS, MRCP,
MRCGP, DCH

Series editors: Anita Ganeri and A. Patricia Sechi
Design: Edward Kinsey
Illustrations: Rhoda and Robert Burns/Drawing Attention
Photography: Chris Fairclough; Zefa
Typesetting: Lineage Ltd, Watford

The publisher would like to thank Thomas Kinsey for
appearing in the photographs of this book.

93-724

CONTENTS

A sunny day

Imagine standing outside on a cold, snowy winter's day – in your swimsuit! Or running around in the summer sun – in your thickest coat! The human body works best and stays healthiest at a steady temperature. Clothes and activities are designed to help keep your body's temperature steady. Your body can control its own inside temperature by natural processes such as sweating and shivering.

△ It's summer vacation time and the weather is warm and sunny. You are off to the beach for the day. No need to take a coat with you!

▷ Your skin is your body's natural "coat." It helps to keep out water, heat and cold, and harmful rays from the sun. Most of your skin is only 1-3 millimeters thick. This is what it looks like under a microscope.

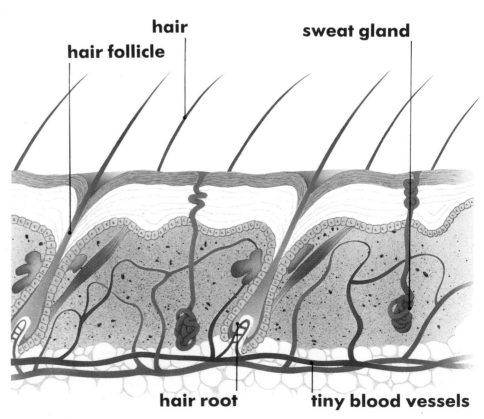

hair

hair follicle

sweat gland

hair root

tiny blood vessels

DIFFERENT TEMPERATURES

Your body works best and feels most comfortable when it has a temperature of 98.6°F. How hot is this compared with your surroundings? Use a thermometer to help you measure the temperatures of various places around you. (Get an adult to help you with this and be very careful not to break the thermometer.) Try your

living room and school classroom. Try outside in the backyard, on a sunny path, or in a shady corner. Write down your results in a notebook. Are any of these places exactly 98.6°F? Your body has to adjust itself as it goes from one place to another, to keep its temperature steady. Wearing suitable clothes plays an important part in this.

TEMPERATURE FACTS

• Temperate lands such as Britain do not have great extremes of temperature throughout the year.
• In the far north of Scandinavia, North America and Siberia, winter temperatures drop far below freezing, to −40°F or even lower. These temperatures last for weeks on end.
• People in those places must live in well-insulated houses and wear extra-warm clothes.
• In the desert sun of the Sahara, midday temperatures can reach a scorching 120°F. This is almost 22°F warmer than your body.
• People there wear loose robes and hoods that protect them from the sun's glare, but which allow air to move around their bodies and cool them down.

Too hot?

△ As you run about in the sun, your body gets too hot. One of its ways of cooling itself down is by sweating.

▷ Sweat glands are tiny knots of tubes in your skin. They make watery sweat, or perspiration. When you get too hot, sweat oozes up each tube and out of a tiny hole, called a sweat pore, on to your skin. As it dries, it draws heat from your body.

Your body keeps warm by making its own heat. Its natural chemical processes, especially those involved in muscle power, create heat. There are always muscles at work in your body. Your muscular heart beats, and muscles in your intestines push food along. If you move about, muscles in your arms and legs make even more heat. Warm air also makes you hot. On a summer day, when the air is too warm to cool your body, you may get too hot. Your body then has to cool itself down.

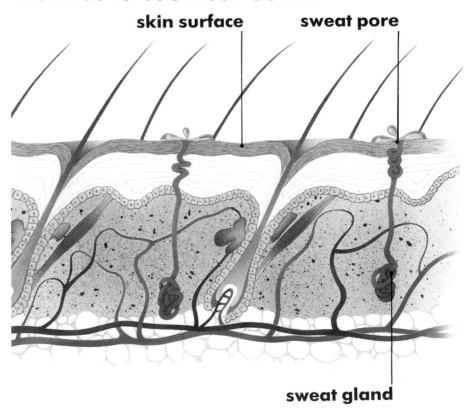

skin surface   **sweat pore**

sweat gland

SWEAT FACTS

- Certain patches of skin have more sweat glands than others. These areas are shown on the right.
- Adults perspire more than children.
- An average person has as many as 3-5 million sweat glands over the whole body.
- Even in cool conditions, sweat glands release about half a liter, or 1 quart, of sweat each day.

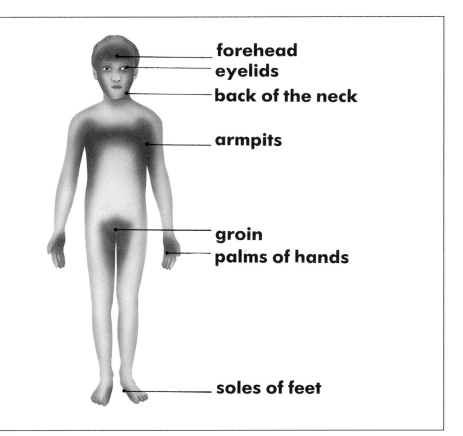

forehead
eyelids
back of the neck

armpits

groin
palms of hands

soles of feet

HOW COOLING IS SWEAT?

Sweat cools your body by evaporation. This is when water turns from a liquid into an invisible gas, called water vapor. Heat from your body is needed for the water in sweat to evaporate. Try this experiment to see how evaporation draws heat from your body and cools you down. Sit in a sunny, breezy place. Place a damp towel over one bare leg, and a dry towel over the other. As the water in the damp towel evaporates, it draws heat away from your body. It should make that leg feel cooler than the leg with the dry towel.

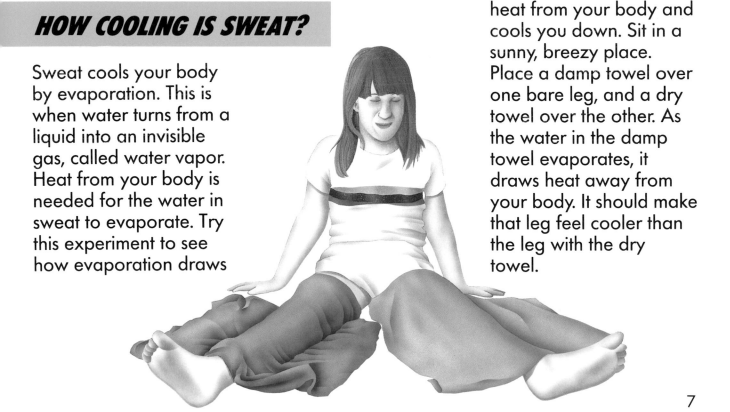

MAKING SWEAT

Sweat is not just made up of water. It also contains sodium chloride (better known as salt), and waste body chemicals, such as urea, and lactic acid. Try making your own "sweat" sample by stirring a teaspoon of ordinary table salt into a quart of warm water. Sip a tiny bit of the liquid. It probably tastes horrible! As sweat

dries on your body, it leaves the salt and other chemicals behind on your skin. If you lick the skin on your arm, for example, after you have been sweating, you may notice a salty taste. Regular washing helps to remove the sweat and chemicals from your skin and stops your body from smelling.

COOL FLUSH

Your blood spreads heat around your body, just as the hot water in central-heating pipes spreads heat around a house. When your body is too hot, tiny blood vessels in your skin become wider. They can now carry more blood. This means that more heat from your blood can pass through your skin into the air, cooling your body down. In a light-skinned person, the

wider blood vessels near the skin's surface gives the skin a pinkish color, especially on the cheeks. This is called flushing or blushing.

narrow blood vessel near skin, less heat lost

wide blood vessel near skin, lots of heat lost

AUTOMATIC CONTROL

Sweating and flushing happen automatically. You don't have to think about them. Part of your brain, called the brain stem, sends nerve signals into a special network, called the autonomic nervous system. (This is different from the nerves that control your muscles and movements.) Its nerves tell sweat glands to release sweat, and blood vessels to widen.

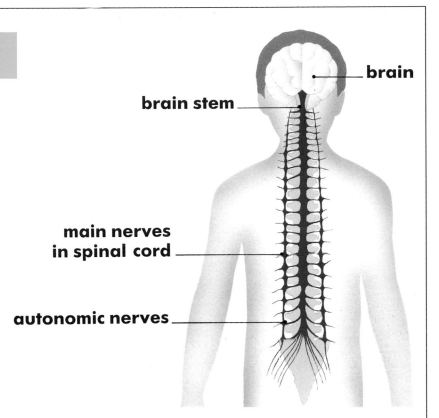

brain

brain stem

main nerves in spinal cord

autonomic nerves

TOO HOT TO BE HEALTHY

Too much hot sun can be very harmful. It drains your body of precious fluids so that it cannot sweat and keep cool. The rising temperature also affects your brain's temperature-control center. Very high body temperature is called hyperthermia, and needs medical care. People working in hot places use awnings or tents to keep them cool.

In for a swim

△ A swim is cooling and refreshing. The natural oils in your skin keep it from becoming waterlogged.

One way of cooling down is to go for a swim in the cool ocean. Warmth from your body passes out through your skin and into the water. If you keep moving, your body does not have time to warm up the water around it. The flow of cool water helps cool you down even more. Being in the ocean shows another feature of your skin. It prevents water from getting inside you. This is because it has an oily surface that keeps out water. Your skin also keeps precious fluids from leaking out of your body.

▷ Skin is waterproofed by a natural oily substance, called sebum. This is made by tiny sebaceous glands near each hair. The sebum oozes up the hole in which the hair grows, and spreads onto your skin. It keeps your skin soft and supple.

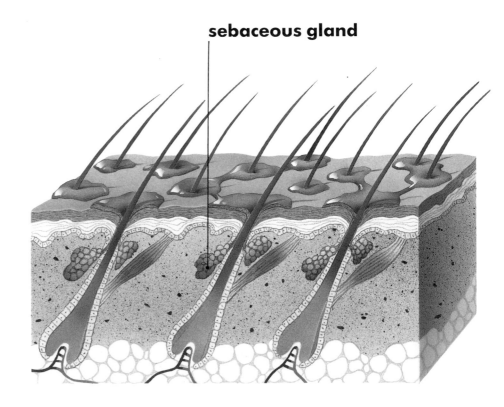

sebaceous gland

WATERPROOFING FACTS

otter

dugong

duck

- Human skin is "showerproof" rather than being completely waterproof. If you stayed in water for several hours, your skin would eventually become soggy and waterlogged.
- Animals that live in or spend most of their lives in water have much better waterproofing than we do.
- The dugong, a sea mammal, has a thick skin that is rich in waterproofing oils.
- An otter's dense fur is also rich in natural oils, like sebum, that keep water out.
- Water birds such as ducks, geese and swans often preen their feathers with their beaks. This spreads waterproofing oils all over their feathers and skin.

HOW IS WATER KEPT OUT?

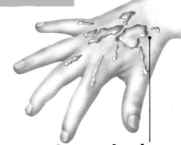

recently washed, oil-free skin

skin with natural oils

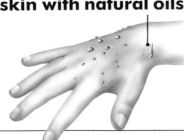

Oily, greasy and waxy substances all help to repel water. At the end of the day, your hands may be covered in grease and dirt, as well as natural skin oils. At the sink, turn on the cold water and let it run over your hand. Do the droplets roll along, without soaking in? Now wash your hands thoroughly with soap and warm water to remove the natural oils. Then dry them. Try again with droplets of water. Does your skin keep them out so well this time? Rub a thin layer of moisturizing cream or petroleum jelly over your hands, and try the droplets of water again. How well do the extra oil and grease repel water?

Too cold?

△ You've spent too much time in the water and now you feel cold! Time to get dry and dressed, until you get warmed up again.

Just as your body tries to cool down when it is too hot, it also tries to warm up when it is too cold. Sensors inside your body detect its fall in temperature, and your brain's temperature-control system switches on the warming processes. These work in an automatic way, like the cooling processes of sweating and flushing. You may also feel colder, and put on extra clothes to help warm yourself up.

▷ Different parts of your body lose heat at different rates. Most heat is lost from your head, although this depends on how much hair you have! Much heat is also lost through your hands and feet. They have a large skin surface for their size.

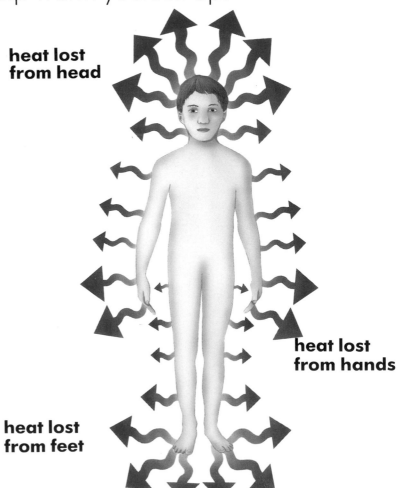

heat lost from head

heat lost from hands

heat lost from feet

A LAYER OF FAT

Under your skin there is a layer of fat, called subcutaneous fat. Fat is a good insulator — it stops heat (or cold) from passing through it. Your fat layer is only about 1/8 to 1/4 inch thick. In whales that live in cold oceans, though, the fat (called blubber) is *4* inches thick!

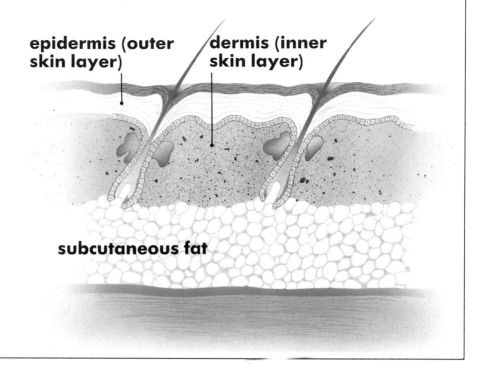

epidermis (outer skin layer)

dermis (inner skin layer)

subcutaneous fat

COLD FACTS

• One of the body's reactions to being too cold is shivering. Shivering muscles twitch automatically. You don't have to think about controlling them. Sometimes it is quite difficult to stop them!

• The chemical processes and movements of shivering muscles generate heat that warms up the body.

• Parts of the body that usually shiver are the forearms and hands,
thighs, and jaw muscles.

• As your jaw moves it makes your teeth click together very quickly. This is what happens when you say your teeth are "chattering."

• In freezing weather, parts of the body that are not protected may freeze, too. The blood and body fluids under the skin turn solid. This is called frostbite and needs urgent medical care.

• The body's extremities — fingers, toes, nose and ears — are the parts most at risk to frostbite.

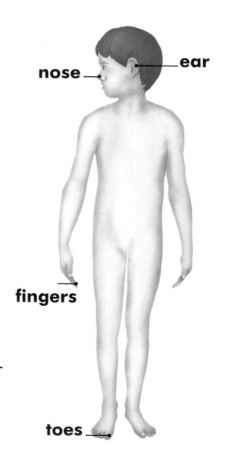

nose

ear

fingers

toes

KEEPING HEAT IN

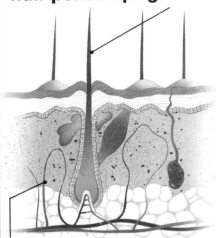

hair pulled upright

narrowed blood vessels

Two other automatic reactions help keep heat in. The first is the opposite to flushing (see page 8). Tiny blood vessels near your skin's surface get narrower and can carry less blood. This means less heat is lost through your skin. The second reaction is your hair standing on end.

Tiny muscles pull the hairs upright. This helps to trap air, a good insulator, near the skin. This reaction is not very effective in humans, though, since our body hairs are so small and fine. It works better in animals and birds. They fluff up their thick fur and feathers to keep themselves warm.

WHY IS WOOL WARM?

Wooly or furry material traps air, which is a good insulator. It can insulate from both heat and cold. Sit in the warm sun and place a piece of thin material, such as a cotton dish towel, over one bare leg. Put a piece of furry or wooly material, such as a small rug, over your other leg. Can you feel the heat of the sun equally on both legs? The leg under the thin material probably feels warmer, since the wooly

wooly rug

cotton dish towel

material is insulating your leg from the sun's rays.

TOO COLD TO BE HEALTHY

If the human body gets too cold, its warming processes cannot cope. Usually when you get cold, you feel the need to put on more clothes. But the falling temperature may affect the brain's temperature-control center. The body's warming reactions may get switched off. The brain and mind become confused. You cannot think straight, or sense the extreme cold, or realize the need for extra clothes

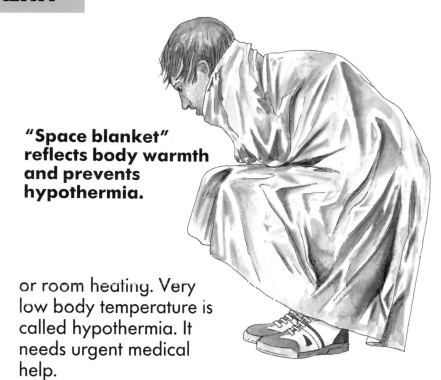

"Space blanket" reflects body warmth and prevents hypothermia.

or room heating. Very low body temperature is called hypothermia. It needs urgent medical help.

GETTING WARM AGAIN

A hot drink soon makes you feel warm inside, even when it still feels cold outside. You can feel these differences in temperature because your body has different temperature sensors. Those in your skin detect your skin's own temperature and that of your body's surroundings. This outer temperature is called the peripheral temperature. Other sensors buried deep inside your body detect the inner, or core, temperature. It may be several degrees higher than the peripheral temperature. When your core temperature begins to fall, you may find yourself at risk for hypothermia (see above).

A refreshing drink

When you sweat, your body loses water. It also loses water when you breathe. Exhaled air contains moisture that has evaporated from inside your airways and lungs. Your body also loses water in its waste products of urine and feces. This water must be replaced regularly, by foods and drinks. Otherwise your body fluids could become too thick and concentrated, and make you ill.

△ Back at the beach, you are getting hot again. You have a refreshing drink to replace fluids lost through sweating.

▷ On an average day, an average person can lose about 1½ quarts of water, in four main ways. These are by sweating, in exhaled air, in chemical waste, such as urine, and in digestive waste, such as feces.

**exhaled
0.3 quarts**

**sweat
0.5 quarts**

**urine
0.6 quarts**

**feces
0.1 quarts**

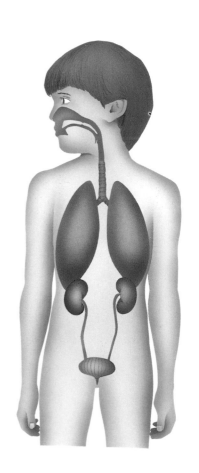

BODY FLUID FACTS

● Your body is about two-thirds water! This means, if you weigh 66 pounds, you have about 44 pounds of water inside you.

● 44 pounds in weight is equivalent to 20 quarts in volume. This is enough to fill 60 soda cans.

● Some parts of the body, such as the blood, are almost entirely water.

● Even hard, strong parts like the bones are one-third water.

● If you drink extra fluids, your kidneys filter the extra water from the blood. It comes out of the body as extra urine.

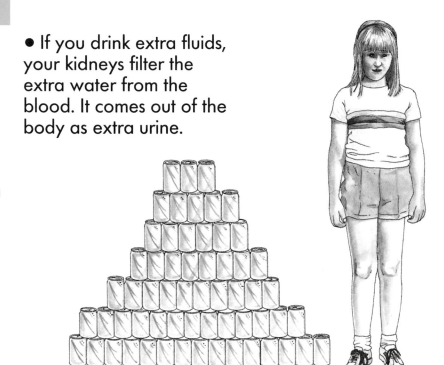

LIFE-SAVING FLUIDS

Some illnesses can make you lose too much water, along with natural body salts and minerals. These include infections of the digestive system, such as gastroenteritis, cholera and dysentery, where symptoms include vomiting and diarrhea. Lack of body fluids is called dehydration, and it can kill. One form of treatment is to replace the lost fluids with a special drink, which contains clean water and the main minerals and salts. This is called oral rehydration therapy. It has already saved the lives of millions of people all around the world.

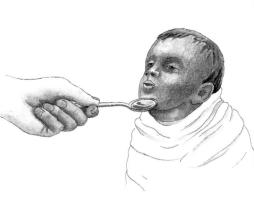

Care in the sun

△ There are many different types of skin color. Your skin color is mainly inherited from your parents.

The sun gives out heat to keep us warm, and light rays for us to see by. It also gives out other kinds of rays. Some of these can be harmful. They include ultraviolet rays, or UV light, which is invisible to our eyes. Too much UV light can damage your skin, causing wrinkles, spots, growths and even skin cancers. Light-skinned people are more likely to be affected than dark-skinned people. This is because they do not have as much of the brown pigment (coloring), melanin, in their skin. Melanin absorbs some of the UV rays so they do not harm the skin.

▷ Skin color is caused by tiny specks of a brownish substance, called melanin. This is made by special cells, called melanocytes, near the surface of your skin. It is taken up and spread by other skin cells, to give an even color.

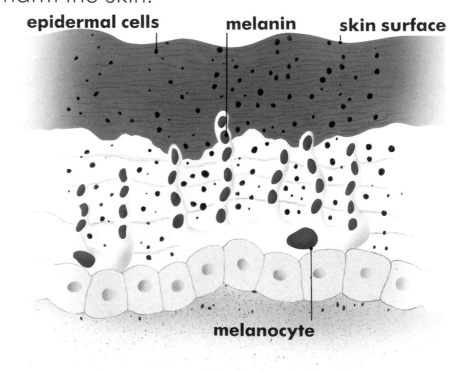

epidermal cells · melanin · skin surface

melanocyte

THE UV FILTER

High above the earth's surface, 12 to 19 miles up, is a layer of gas called ozone. (Ozone is a form of oxygen.) This filters out much of the sun's harmful UV light rays. Industrial chemicals and air pollution are damaging the ozone layer. In some places, such as

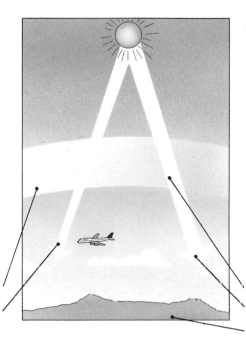

ozone layer

UV rays

thin ozone layer
more UV rays
earth's surface

Antarctica, the damage is so bad that scientists have discovered thin patches in the ozone layer. Unless this stops, the ozone layer will let more UV light through. People below will be at greater risk of developing skin problems, such as growths and cancers.

TAKING CARE IN THE SUN

You should always take care of your skin whenever you go out in the sun. This is especially important on the first few days of a vacation in a hot, sunny place. Don't spend too long in the sun on your first day or you run the risk of getting badly sunburned. An hour is probably long enough. As you get used to the sun, you can build up gradually, spending longer in the sun each day. Always keep out of the strong midday sun. You might not realize how strong it actually is. It is a good idea to wear a sunhat to protect your head, apply plenty of sunblock and use an umbrella for a bit of welcome shade.

LIGHT AND DARK

An object's color and texture affect how much heat it absorbs. Dark things, and those with dull or rough surfaces, take up heat quickly. Light things, and those with shiny surfaces, tend to reflect heat away. They warm up more slowly. This is why it is more comfortable to wear light-colored clothes in

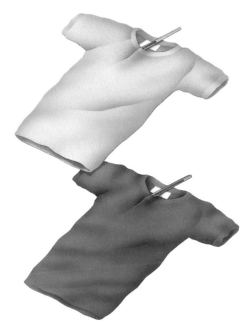

hot places. You can see how this works using two t-shirts — one black or very dark, and the other white or very light in color. Put them in the refrigerator for an hour. Then lay them side by side in the hot sun. Take the temperature inside each shirt with a thermometer, every 5 minutes. Which t-shirt warms up fastest?

ARTIFICIAL SUN

Some people like to get a tan by lying under sunlamps. These give out heat, light and UV rays, just like the real sun. They can cause just the same problems as the real sun and this type of sunbathing must only be done in a careful and controlled way, so that the skin is not harmed. Some types of sunlamps have now been designed to give out less of the harmful UV rays.

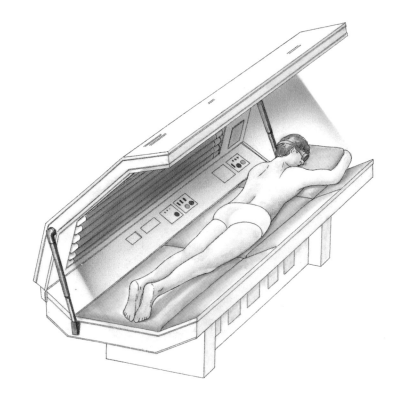

Too much sun

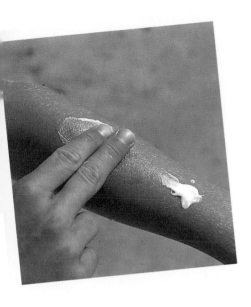

△ At the start of a hot sunny vacation you should always use a sunscreen. This will help to protect your skin until it gets used to the sunshine.

If your skin is suddenly exposed to too much sunshine, it may become red, swollen and sore. This causes the hot, burning feeling we call sunburn. The sun's UV rays are the main cause of sunburn. People who have not been exposed to the sun for a long time are most at risk. If you spend a sensible' amount of time in the sun, your skin may make more melanin, to protect itself naturally. Your skin gradually turns darker. This is called a suntan.

▷ Unprotected skin reacts to strong sunshine and UV light by becoming inflamed. It swells and fills with fluid, and feels hot and sore. Inflammation is a natural reaction of your body's defense system.

healthy skin

sunburned skin

skin before sunburn

swollen skin

redness

SUNBURN FACTS

- Mild sunburn makes the skin sore and red. But severe sunburn can be extremely painful, even life-threatening.
- People with light skin and fair hair are usually most at risk from sunburn.
- Dark-skinned people have some natural protection from the sun because their skin makes more melanin. But they should also take care in the sun.

- UV rays are not only in bright sunlight, they can pass through hazy cloud.
- Sunscreen creams and lotions help to protect the skin. The higher the SPF (Sun Protection Factor), the more protection they give. SPFs of 15 or more are reasonably high.

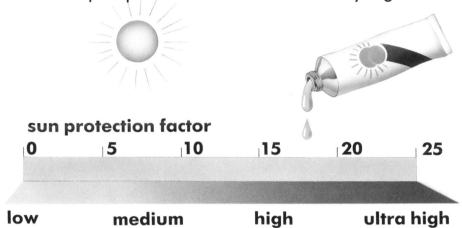

sun protection factor

0	5	10	15	20	25
low		medium		high	ultra high

A HEALTHY TAN?

Many years ago, in places like Europe and North America, it was thought fashionable for light-skinned people to have very pale skin. This was seen as proof that they were wealthy. They did not have to work in the fields, where they would get tanned by the sun. Later it became fashionable for people to have a suntan. This also showed they were wealthy. They had money to go on vacation to exotic, hot places. A person with a suntan was seen as "glowing with health." Today, we know that too much sun can be harmful.

FRECKLES AND MOLES

Some people have skin that is not quite the same color all over. For example, freckles are small patches of slightly darker skin. They are due to extra melanocytes clumped together in each patch. Exposure to the sun makes the melanocytes in the freckles produce more melanin, as in a normal suntan. So the freckle "suntans" more than the surrounding skin, and looks much darker. A mole is a dense, concentrated patch of melanocytes, which make lots of melanin. In the condition known as albinism, a person's melanocytes cannot make melanin. That person's hair and skin are almost white. He or she has very little protection from sunburn and must be very careful.

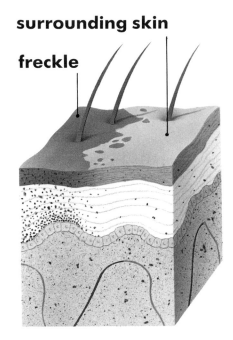

surrounding skin

freckle

HEALTH WARNINGS

The dangers of skin cancers and other diseases caused by too much sunlight, are now well known. In Australia, for example, skin cancer is one of the most common illnesses there is. In places such as Australia, South Africa and California, there are now posters, advertisements and medical advice warning people about the dangers of sun-related skin diseases.

Looking cool

Bright sunlight can also affect your eyes. Normally, the hole at the front of each eye, called the pupil, becomes smaller in bright light. This prevents too much light from entering the eye. But if the rays are very strong, they could damage the sensitive back of your eye, called the retina. Wearing sunglasses can help cut down the amount of bright light and also ease eyestrain.

△ The glare of the afternoon sun on the waves and sand is too strong. Sunglasses help to shade your eyes.

1 Half fill the eyebath cup with eyewash.

2 Place it firmly over your eye, and tilt your head backward.

▷ Hot, tired eyes can be soothed by an eyebath. The bath also helps to wash away windblown sand and dust. Follow the instructions on the leaflet or container. Take good care of your eyes. Sight is a precious sense.

3 Blink to let the fluid wash over the surface of your eye. Repeat on the other eye.

24

GLARING FACTS

- Bright light can reflect off snow, sand and water, giving flashes and patches of even stronger light known as "glare."
- Skiers and other people in the snow may have their sight damaged by too much glare from the white snow. This is called snow blindness.

- Mild snow blindness usually gets better. But many people wear dark goggles to prevent it.
- Some people depend on good eyesight in awkward conditions, like pilots and long-distance truck drivers. They usually wear sunglasses to reduce glare and eyestrain.

WHAT TYPE OF SUNGLASSES?

There are several types of sunglasses. One type simply has darker lenses to reduce the amount of light your eyes receive. Another type has polarized lenses. These filter out certain kinds of light rays and stop glare.

A third type has photochromatic lenses. These react to the level of light. They are clear in dull conditions, and turn dark in bright sunlight. You can test to see if a lens is polarized, by holding it on top of a lens

that you *know* is polarized. Look through both lenses and rotate one of them. If both lenses are polarized, the amount of light coming through should be reduced to almost nothing as you turn the lens.

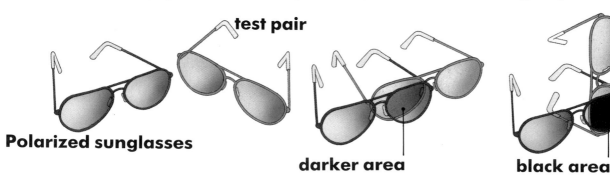

test pair

Polarized sunglasses

darker area

black area

A cooling breeze

As your body gives off heat to the surrounding air, it warms this air. The warmed air doesn't cool you down, but if this air moves away and is replaced by cooler air again, you may feel colder. Wind is moving air, so it cools your body down more than still air. A cooling breeze is very welcome on a hot day. But on a cold day, a cold wind can make you much too chilly, unless you are well wrapped up in warm, windproof clothes.

△ If there is no wind, make some! Fan yourself to blow cooling air past your skin.

▷ Body heat is kept in by a large bulk, or volume. It is lost by a large surface area. The body of a child usually has a small volume and a relatively large surface. So it cools faster than an adult's body, which is much bigger in volume, but only slightly larger in surface area.

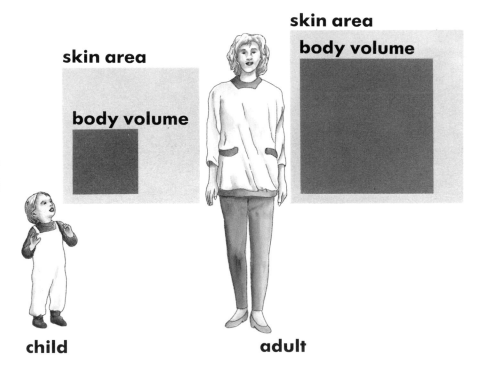

skin area

body volume

child

skin area

body volume

adult

WIND FACTS

- The fastest wind ever recorded was blowing at 230 miles per hour. It was blowing 6,560 feet up on a high mountainside.
- A cold wind that blows heat away from the body makes the air feel cooler than it really is. This is called the wind chill factor.
- People out walking in a cold wind can experience a wind chill temperature 15-20 degrees lower than the true air temperature. They need windproof clothes and hoods.
- Humidity, the amount of water vapor in the air, also affects body cooling. Very humid air cannot evaporate sweat easily from the body, so you tend to feel hot and "sticky."

HOW COOL IS THE WIND?

Show how wind has a cooling effect using a jar of water. Take the temperature of the water with a thermometer. Then leave the jar in the hot sun on a breezy day. Use a cardboard "windbreak" to stop most of the wind, but make sure the sun can still shine on the jar. Leave it for about 20 minutes, then take the temperature of the water again. Now remove the windbreak so the breeze can blow over the glass. If the breeze drops, or for better results, use a fan, too. Leave it for 20 minutes, then take the temperature of the water again. Has it changed?

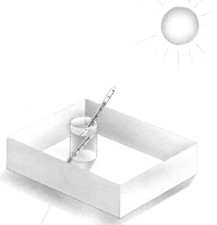

Things to do

CURLING UP TO KEEP WARM

When you feel cold, your natural reaction may be to curl up into a ball shape. This helps to keep warmth inside your body, as the ball shape gives only a small surface area from which to lose heat. When you are hot, you tend to do the opposite and stretch yourself out to lose heat.

See how this works with a piece of aluminum foil and a thermometer. Ask an adult to help you. Fold the foil and put it in a sink of warm water. Take it out after a few minutes and wrap the middle of the foil around the thermometer. Put it in a cool place and record its temperature every minute for 10 minutes. Repeat the experiment but this time crush the foil into a ball shape when you take it out of the water. Does the foil lose heat faster as a flat sheet or as a curled-up ball?

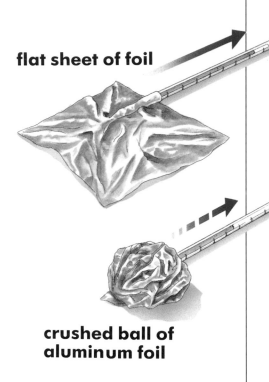

flat sheet of foil

crushed ball of aluminum foil

TEMPERATURES AROUND THE WORLD

Find out how warm or cold various places in the world are. Look in vacation brochures or atlases for charts showing how temperatures change throughout the year. Start with big cities, such as Los Angeles, New York, Rio de Janeiro, London,

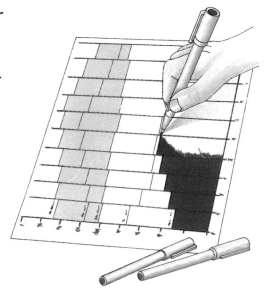

Madrid, Cairo, Nairobi, Moscow, Delhi, Sydney, Beijing, and Tokyo. Draw a graph of the temperatures, like the one here, and mark your own area's temperature on it. Then mark the temperature of the human body, 98.6°F. Which places are hotter than this?

SUN POWER

The sun gives out huge amounts of heat and light. These are forms of energy. Look around your home, school and neighborhood for things powered by the sun. Do you have a solar-powered calculator or watch? Some buildings have solar panels on their roofs, to use the sun's energy to make electricity and heat water.

ULTRAVIOLET LIGHT

If you live in a hot, sunny place, you may already know about the problems of UV light. In general, too much UV light harms the skin. But it is not quite as simple as this. There are at least two types of UV light, called UV-A and UV-B. One type is the burning rays that tend to cause sunburn. The other is the aging rays that make the skin creased and wrinkled, as in old age. Look out for leaflets, especially in sports and fitness centers where there are sunbeds for rent.

THE SUNBATHING BUSINESS

Pay a visit to your local drugstore or supermarket and look at all the products to do with sunbathing. Spring or early summer are the best times to do this, when people are preparing for their vacations and there are lots of products on sale. What information do the containers give about care in the sun? What is the difference between a suntan lotion and a sunscreen? Do some of these lotions stay on while you are swimming? What are the highest and lowest SPFs (Sun Protection Factors) you can find?

WEATHER WATCHING

Look at the weather forecasts in the newspapers and listen to them on the radio and television. Do they mention temperatures, wind speed and wind chill factors? Places where wind chill is important are usually very cold and windy. The forecasts for ski resorts and mountain-climbing centers are most likely to give information about wind chill.

Glossary

Blood   A red liquid that flows around and around the body inside tubes, called blood vessels. It carries oxygen, nutrients and energy-containing substances from digested foods.

Brain   A large, tangled mass of interconnected nerves inside the head. It is the control center of the body, and other nerves link it to the various body parts.

Brain stem   The lower part of the brain, which controls automatic processes such as heartbeat, breathing, sweating and shivering.

Core temperature   The temperature deep in the middle of the head or body, which may be slightly different from the temperature of the skin.

Dermis   The lower layer of skin, below the epidermis. It contains skin sensors, blood vessels, nerves and elastic fibers.

Epidermis   The outer surface layer of skin, above the dermis. It is mostly tough and dead, and resists wear and rubbing.

Hyperthermia   When the body's temperature becomes dangerously high, as in "heat stroke."

Hypothermia   When the body's temperature becomes dangerously low, as in "exposure."

Insulator   A substance that prevents heat (or electricity) from passing through it. Body fat is a good heat insulator.

Melanin   A brown-colored substance (pigment) made by special cells, called melanocytes, in the skin. It is in the form of microscopic grains or granules. More melanin makes the skin color darker.

Muscle   A body part specialized for becoming shorter (contracting). As it does so, it pulls on the bone, muscle, or other body parts to which it is fixed.

Retina   The layer lining the inside of the rear of the eye. It detects light rays and turns them into nerve signals.

Sebaceous gland   A microscopic structure in the skin, next to a hair. It makes the natural skin oil called sebum.

Subcutaneous   Meaning under the skin. The subcutaneous fat layer is a layer of fatty substance just under the dermis.

Sweat   A watery liquid made by microscopic structures in the skin, called sweat glands. Sweat contains body salts and minerals, and it helps to cool the body.

UV light   Ultraviolet light. The eyes cannot see it, but if it is too strong, it can damage the body, especially the skin.

Urine   A watery fluid that the kidneys make by filtering the blood. It contains waste substances from the body's thousands of chemical reactions.

Resources

BOOKS

The Human Body by Gilda Berger
(New York: Doubleday, 1989)

Fascinating Body Facts by Giles Brandreth
(New York: Sterling, 1987)

The Human Body by D. Bruun and Bertel Bruun
(New York: Random House, 1982)

Macmillan Book of the Human Body by Mary Elting
(New York: Macmillan, 1986)

Why Does My Nose Run? And Other Questions Kids Ask About Their Bodies by Joanne Settel and Nancy Baggett
(New York: Atheneum, 1985)

Index